50 Low-Fat Dishes for Light and Healthy Meals

By: Kelly Johnson

Table of Contents

- Grilled Lemon Herb Chicken Salad
- Baked Salmon with Asparagus
- Veggie Stir-Fry with Tofu
- Zucchini Noodles with Marinara Sauce
- Quinoa and Black Bean Salad
- Spaghetti Squash with Garlic and Olive Oil
- Roasted Cauliflower and Chickpea Bowl
- Grilled Shrimp with Avocado Salsa
- Baked Sweet Potato with Greek Yogurt
- Cabbage and Carrot Slaw
- Turkey Lettuce Wraps
- Broiled Tilapia with Steamed Vegetables
- Eggplant Parmesan (Light Version)
- Chickpea and Spinach Curry
- Cauliflower Fried Rice
- Grilled Portobello Mushrooms
- Shrimp and Vegetable Skewers
- Spicy Roasted Brussels Sprouts
- Grilled Chicken with Quinoa Salad
- Cucumber and Tomato Salad with Balsamic
- Baked Chicken with Sweet Potato Fries
- Spaghetti with Turkey Meatballs
- Roasted Zucchini with Garlic and Basil
- Mediterranean Hummus and Veggie Wrap
- Lemon Garlic Tilapia
- Greek Salad with Grilled Chicken
- Stuffed Bell Peppers with Quinoa and Veggies
- Sautéed Shrimp with Spinach
- Grilled Veggie and Hummus Pita
- Baked Eggplant with Tomato and Basil
- Sweet Potato and Kale Soup
- Broccoli and Almond Salad
- Grilled Lemon Chicken with Steamed Broccoli
- Zesty Tomato and Basil Soup
- Cauliflower and Broccoli Fritters

- Grilled Salmon with Avocado Salsa
- Tofu Stir-Fry with Veggies
- Cabbage and Bean Soup
- Lemon Herb Grilled Vegetables
- Turkey Chili
- Spinach and Feta Stuffed Chicken Breast
- Carrot and Ginger Soup
- Roasted Beet and Goat Cheese Salad
- Sautéed Spinach and Garlic with Lemon
- Light Chicken Fajitas
- Baked Cod with Veggie Medley
- Grilled Shrimp with Cucumber Relish
- Spicy Chicken and Cabbage Stir-Fry
- Cauliflower and Lentil Stew
- Grilled Tuna Salad with Lime Vinaigrette

Grilled Lemon Herb Chicken Salad

Ingredients:

- 2 chicken breasts
- 1 lemon (zested and juiced)
- 2 tbsp olive oil
- 1 tbsp fresh oregano, chopped
- 1 tbsp fresh thyme, chopped
- 1 garlic clove, minced
- Salt and pepper to taste
- 4 cups mixed greens (arugula, spinach, etc.)
- 1 cucumber, sliced
- 1/4 red onion, thinly sliced
- 1/4 cup feta cheese, crumbled (optional)

Instructions:

1. Preheat the grill to medium-high heat.
2. In a small bowl, combine lemon juice, lemon zest, olive oil, oregano, thyme, garlic, salt, and pepper.
3. Coat the chicken breasts with the marinade and let sit for 10-15 minutes.
4. Grill the chicken for 6-7 minutes per side until fully cooked.
5. Slice the grilled chicken and serve on top of mixed greens, cucumber, red onion, and feta.
6. Drizzle with extra dressing if desired and serve.

Baked Salmon with Asparagus

Ingredients:

- 2 salmon fillets
- 1 bunch asparagus, trimmed
- 2 tbsp olive oil
- 1 lemon, sliced
- 1 garlic clove, minced
- Salt and pepper to taste
- Fresh dill (optional)

Instructions:

1. Preheat the oven to 400°F (200°C).
2. Place salmon fillets on a baking sheet lined with parchment paper.
3. Arrange asparagus around the salmon.
4. Drizzle olive oil over the salmon and asparagus.
5. Sprinkle with minced garlic, salt, and pepper.
6. Top with lemon slices and fresh dill if using.
7. Bake for 12-15 minutes, or until the salmon is cooked through.
8. Serve hot with a side of roasted vegetables or rice.

Veggie Stir-Fry with Tofu

Ingredients:

- 1 block firm tofu, drained and cubed
- 1 tbsp sesame oil
- 1/2 onion, thinly sliced
- 1 bell pepper, sliced
- 1 zucchini, sliced
- 1 carrot, julienned
- 1 cup broccoli florets
- 2 tbsp soy sauce
- 1 tbsp hoisin sauce
- 1 tbsp rice vinegar
- 1 tbsp fresh ginger, grated
- 1 garlic clove, minced
- Sesame seeds for garnish

Instructions:

1. Press tofu to remove excess water, then cut into cubes.
2. In a large skillet, heat sesame oil over medium heat.
3. Add tofu and cook until golden and crispy on all sides.
4. Remove tofu and set aside.
5. In the same skillet, add onion, bell pepper, zucchini, carrot, and broccoli. Stir-fry for 5-7 minutes until veggies are tender.
6. Add soy sauce, hoisin sauce, rice vinegar, ginger, and garlic to the veggies. Stir to combine.
7. Return tofu to the skillet and toss everything together.
8. Serve with rice or noodles and sprinkle with sesame seeds.

Zucchini Noodles with Marinara Sauce

Ingredients:

- 4 medium zucchinis, spiralized into noodles
- 1 tbsp olive oil
- 2 cups marinara sauce
- 1 garlic clove, minced
- 1/4 cup fresh basil, chopped
- Salt and pepper to taste
- Grated Parmesan cheese for garnish (optional)

Instructions:

1. Heat olive oil in a large skillet over medium heat.
2. Add garlic and sauté until fragrant.
3. Add marinara sauce and simmer for 5-7 minutes.
4. Add zucchini noodles to the skillet and toss with the sauce. Cook for 2-3 minutes until noodles are tender.
5. Season with salt and pepper.
6. Garnish with fresh basil and Parmesan cheese.
7. Serve immediately as a healthy, low-carb pasta alternative.

Quinoa and Black Bean Salad

Ingredients:

- 1 cup quinoa, cooked
- 1 can (15 oz) black beans, drained and rinsed
- 1/2 red bell pepper, diced
- 1/2 red onion, diced
- 1/4 cup cilantro, chopped
- 1 lime, juiced
- 2 tbsp olive oil
- Salt and pepper to taste
- 1/2 tsp cumin (optional)

Instructions:

1. Cook quinoa according to package instructions and let cool.
2. In a large bowl, combine quinoa, black beans, bell pepper, red onion, and cilantro.
3. In a small bowl, whisk together lime juice, olive oil, salt, pepper, and cumin.
4. Pour the dressing over the salad and toss to combine.
5. Serve chilled or at room temperature.

Spaghetti Squash with Garlic and Olive Oil

Ingredients:

- 1 medium spaghetti squash
- 2 tbsp olive oil
- 3 cloves garlic, minced
- 1/4 cup fresh parsley, chopped
- Salt and pepper to taste
- Grated Parmesan cheese for garnish (optional)

Instructions:

1. Preheat the oven to 400°F (200°C).
2. Cut the spaghetti squash in half and remove the seeds.
3. Drizzle with olive oil, sprinkle with salt and pepper, and place cut-side down on a baking sheet.
4. Roast for 40-45 minutes, or until the squash is tender and can be shredded into strands.
5. Use a fork to scrape the squash into spaghetti-like strands.
6. Heat olive oil in a pan over medium heat and sauté garlic until fragrant.
7. Toss the spaghetti squash with the garlic oil, parsley, and Parmesan if using.
8. Serve warm.

Roasted Cauliflower and Chickpea Bowl

Ingredients:

- 1 head cauliflower, cut into florets
- 1 can (15 oz) chickpeas, drained and rinsed
- 2 tbsp olive oil
- 1 tsp cumin
- 1/2 tsp turmeric
- Salt and pepper to taste
- 1/4 cup tahini
- 2 tbsp lemon juice
- 1 tbsp water

Instructions:

1. Preheat oven to 400°F (200°C).
2. Toss cauliflower florets and chickpeas with olive oil, cumin, turmeric, salt, and pepper.
3. Spread in a single layer on a baking sheet and roast for 25-30 minutes, or until cauliflower is tender and golden.
4. In a small bowl, whisk together tahini, lemon juice, and water to make a sauce.
5. Serve the roasted cauliflower and chickpeas in a bowl, drizzled with tahini sauce.

Grilled Shrimp with Avocado Salsa

Ingredients:

- 1 lb shrimp, peeled and deveined
- 2 tbsp olive oil
- 1 lime, juiced
- 1 tsp smoked paprika
- Salt and pepper to taste
- 1 avocado, diced
- 1/2 red onion, diced
- 1/4 cup cilantro, chopped
- 1/2 cup cherry tomatoes, halved

Instructions:

1. Preheat the grill to medium-high heat.
2. Toss shrimp with olive oil, lime juice, paprika, salt, and pepper.
3. Grill shrimp for 2-3 minutes per side until fully cooked.
4. While shrimp cooks, mix avocado, red onion, cilantro, and tomatoes in a bowl.
5. Serve shrimp topped with avocado salsa.

Baked Sweet Potato with Greek Yogurt

Ingredients:

- 2 medium sweet potatoes
- 1/2 cup Greek yogurt
- 1 tbsp honey
- 1/4 tsp cinnamon
- 1/4 cup chopped nuts (optional)
- Salt to taste

Instructions:

1. Preheat the oven to 400°F (200°C).
2. Pierce the sweet potatoes with a fork and bake for 45-60 minutes, or until tender.
3. Slice open and top with Greek yogurt, honey, cinnamon, and chopped nuts.
4. Serve as a healthy and filling side dish or light meal.

Cabbage and Carrot Slaw

Ingredients:

- 2 cups shredded cabbage
- 1 cup shredded carrots
- 1/4 cup apple cider vinegar
- 1 tbsp olive oil
- 1 tsp honey
- 1/2 tsp mustard
- Salt and pepper to taste
- 1/4 cup chopped parsley (optional)

Instructions:

1. In a large bowl, combine shredded cabbage and carrots.
2. In a separate small bowl, whisk together apple cider vinegar, olive oil, honey, mustard, salt, and pepper.
3. Pour the dressing over the cabbage and carrots and toss to combine.
4. Garnish with chopped parsley if desired and serve chilled.

Turkey Lettuce Wraps

Ingredients:

- 1 lb ground turkey
- 2 tbsp olive oil
- 1/2 onion, finely chopped
- 2 cloves garlic, minced
- 1/2 bell pepper, finely diced
- 2 tbsp soy sauce
- 1 tbsp hoisin sauce
- 1 tsp fresh ginger, grated
- 1/4 tsp red pepper flakes (optional)
- 1 head iceberg or butter lettuce, leaves separated
- 2 green onions, sliced (for garnish)

Instructions:

1. Heat olive oil in a large skillet over medium heat.
2. Add ground turkey and cook until browned, breaking it apart with a spoon.
3. Add onion, garlic, and bell pepper, and cook until softened.
4. Stir in soy sauce, hoisin sauce, ginger, and red pepper flakes.
5. Cook for an additional 2-3 minutes until everything is well combined.
6. Spoon the turkey mixture into lettuce leaves and garnish with green onions.
7. Serve as a healthy, low-carb meal.

Broiled Tilapia with Steamed Vegetables

Ingredients:

- 2 tilapia fillets
- 1 tbsp olive oil
- 1 lemon, sliced
- 1 tsp garlic powder
- Salt and pepper to taste
- 2 cups mixed vegetables (e.g., broccoli, carrots, zucchini)
- Fresh parsley for garnish

Instructions:

1. Preheat the broiler in your oven.
2. Drizzle olive oil over the tilapia fillets and season with garlic powder, salt, and pepper.
3. Place the fillets under the broiler for 4-5 minutes per side, or until cooked through and flaky.
4. Meanwhile, steam the mixed vegetables until tender (about 5-7 minutes).
5. Serve the tilapia with steamed vegetables and garnish with lemon slices and parsley.

Eggplant Parmesan (Light Version)

Ingredients:

- 1 large eggplant, sliced into rounds
- 1/2 cup whole wheat breadcrumbs
- 1/4 cup grated Parmesan cheese
- 1 cup marinara sauce
- 1/2 cup shredded part-skim mozzarella cheese
- 1/4 cup fresh basil, chopped
- Salt and pepper to taste
- Olive oil spray

Instructions:

1. Preheat the oven to 375°F (190°C).
2. Season eggplant slices with salt and let them sit for 10 minutes to release moisture. Pat dry.
3. In a shallow bowl, combine breadcrumbs and Parmesan cheese.
4. Coat each eggplant slice with the breadcrumb mixture and place on a baking sheet sprayed with olive oil.
5. Bake for 25-30 minutes, flipping halfway through, until crispy and golden.
6. In a baking dish, layer eggplant slices, marinara sauce, and mozzarella.
7. Bake for another 10 minutes until cheese is melted and bubbly.
8. Garnish with fresh basil and serve.

Chickpea and Spinach Curry

Ingredients:

- 1 can (15 oz) chickpeas, drained and rinsed
- 2 cups fresh spinach
- 1 onion, chopped
- 2 cloves garlic, minced
- 1 tbsp fresh ginger, grated
- 1 tbsp curry powder
- 1/2 tsp cumin
- 1/2 tsp turmeric
- 1 can (14 oz) diced tomatoes
- 1/2 cup coconut milk
- Salt and pepper to taste
- Fresh cilantro for garnish

Instructions:

1. Heat olive oil in a large pan over medium heat.
2. Add onion, garlic, and ginger, and sauté until softened.
3. Stir in curry powder, cumin, and turmeric, and cook for 1-2 minutes.
4. Add diced tomatoes, coconut milk, chickpeas, and spinach.
5. Simmer for 10-15 minutes, until the sauce thickens and the spinach wilts.
6. Season with salt and pepper.
7. Garnish with fresh cilantro and serve with rice or naan.

Cauliflower Fried Rice

Ingredients:

- 1 head cauliflower, grated into rice-sized pieces
- 1 tbsp olive oil
- 1/2 onion, diced
- 2 cloves garlic, minced
- 1/2 cup frozen peas and carrots
- 2 eggs, scrambled
- 2 tbsp soy sauce
- 1 tsp sesame oil
- Green onions for garnish

Instructions:

1. In a large skillet, heat olive oil over medium heat.
2. Add onion and garlic, and sauté until softened.
3. Add peas and carrots and cook for 2-3 minutes.
4. Push the vegetables to one side and scramble the eggs on the other side of the pan.
5. Stir in cauliflower rice, soy sauce, and sesame oil.
6. Cook for 5-7 minutes until the cauliflower is tender and resembles fried rice.
7. Garnish with green onions and serve.

Grilled Portobello Mushrooms

Ingredients:

- 4 large Portobello mushrooms, stems removed
- 2 tbsp olive oil
- 2 tbsp balsamic vinegar
- 2 garlic cloves, minced
- 1 tsp dried thyme
- Salt and pepper to taste

Instructions:

1. Preheat the grill to medium-high heat.
2. In a small bowl, whisk together olive oil, balsamic vinegar, garlic, thyme, salt, and pepper.
3. Brush the mushroom caps with the marinade and place them on the grill.
4. Grill for 4-5 minutes per side, until tender and slightly charred.
5. Serve as a side dish or as a vegetarian main course.

Shrimp and Vegetable Skewers

Ingredients:

- 1 lb shrimp, peeled and deveined
- 1 bell pepper, cut into chunks
- 1 zucchini, sliced
- 1 red onion, cut into chunks
- 2 tbsp olive oil
- 1 tbsp lemon juice
- 1 tsp smoked paprika
- Salt and pepper to taste

Instructions:

1. Preheat the grill to medium heat.
2. Thread shrimp, bell pepper, zucchini, and onion onto skewers.
3. Drizzle with olive oil, lemon juice, smoked paprika, salt, and pepper.
4. Grill for 2-3 minutes per side, until shrimp is pink and vegetables are tender.
5. Serve with a side of rice or salad.

Spicy Roasted Brussels Sprouts

Ingredients:

- 1 lb Brussels sprouts, trimmed and halved
- 2 tbsp olive oil
- 1/2 tsp red pepper flakes
- 1/2 tsp garlic powder
- Salt and pepper to taste

Instructions:

1. Preheat the oven to 400°F (200°C).
2. Toss Brussels sprouts with olive oil, red pepper flakes, garlic powder, salt, and pepper.
3. Spread in a single layer on a baking sheet.
4. Roast for 20-25 minutes, tossing halfway through, until crispy and browned.
5. Serve as a side dish.

Grilled Chicken with Quinoa Salad

Ingredients:

- 2 boneless, skinless chicken breasts
- 1 tbsp olive oil
- Salt and pepper to taste
- 1 cup quinoa, cooked
- 1/2 cucumber, diced
- 1/2 red bell pepper, diced
- 1/4 red onion, finely chopped
- 1/4 cup fresh parsley, chopped
- 1 tbsp olive oil (for salad dressing)
- 1 tbsp lemon juice
- 1 tsp Dijon mustard
- 1/2 tsp garlic powder

Instructions:

1. Preheat the grill to medium-high heat.
2. Drizzle chicken breasts with olive oil, season with salt and pepper, and grill for 6-7 minutes per side, or until fully cooked.
3. In a bowl, combine cooked quinoa, cucumber, bell pepper, red onion, and parsley.
4. In a small bowl, whisk together olive oil, lemon juice, Dijon mustard, garlic powder, salt, and pepper.
5. Drizzle dressing over the quinoa salad and toss to combine.
6. Serve the grilled chicken over the quinoa salad.

Cucumber and Tomato Salad with Balsamic

Ingredients:

- 1 cucumber, sliced
- 1 pint cherry tomatoes, halved
- 1/4 red onion, thinly sliced
- 1 tbsp olive oil
- 1 tbsp balsamic vinegar
- 1 tsp honey
- Salt and pepper to taste
- Fresh basil for garnish

Instructions:

1. In a bowl, combine cucumber, cherry tomatoes, and red onion.
2. In a separate bowl, whisk together olive oil, balsamic vinegar, honey, salt, and pepper.
3. Pour the dressing over the vegetables and toss to coat.
4. Garnish with fresh basil and serve chilled.

Baked Chicken with Sweet Potato Fries

Ingredients:

- 2 boneless, skinless chicken breasts
- 2 tbsp olive oil
- Salt and pepper to taste
- 1 tsp paprika
- 2 medium sweet potatoes, peeled and cut into fries
- 1 tbsp olive oil (for fries)
- 1 tsp garlic powder
- 1/2 tsp cumin

Instructions:

1. Preheat the oven to 400°F (200°C).
2. Season chicken breasts with olive oil, salt, pepper, and paprika.
3. Arrange chicken breasts on a baking sheet and bake for 20-25 minutes, or until cooked through.
4. Meanwhile, toss the sweet potato fries with olive oil, garlic powder, cumin, salt, and pepper.
5. Spread fries on another baking sheet in a single layer and bake for 25-30 minutes, flipping halfway through, until crispy.
6. Serve the baked chicken with sweet potato fries.

Spaghetti with Turkey Meatballs

Ingredients:

- 1 lb ground turkey
- 1/4 cup breadcrumbs
- 1/4 cup grated Parmesan cheese
- 1 egg
- 1/4 cup fresh parsley, chopped
- 2 cups marinara sauce
- 1 tsp dried oregano
- Salt and pepper to taste
- 8 oz spaghetti

Instructions:

1. Preheat the oven to 375°F (190°C).
2. In a bowl, combine ground turkey, breadcrumbs, Parmesan, egg, parsley, salt, and pepper.
3. Form into meatballs and place them on a baking sheet.
4. Bake for 15-20 minutes, or until cooked through.
5. Meanwhile, cook spaghetti according to package instructions.
6. Heat marinara sauce in a large pan over medium heat, add meatballs, and simmer for 5 minutes.
7. Serve meatballs and sauce over the spaghetti.

Roasted Zucchini with Garlic and Basil

Ingredients:

- 2 zucchinis, sliced
- 1 tbsp olive oil
- 2 cloves garlic, minced
- Salt and pepper to taste
- Fresh basil leaves, chopped

Instructions:

1. Preheat the oven to 400°F (200°C).
2. Toss zucchini slices with olive oil, minced garlic, salt, and pepper.
3. Arrange zucchini on a baking sheet in a single layer.
4. Roast for 15-20 minutes, flipping halfway through, until tender and lightly browned.
5. Garnish with fresh basil and serve.

Mediterranean Hummus and Veggie Wrap

Ingredients:

- 4 whole wheat tortillas
- 1 cup hummus
- 1/2 cucumber, sliced
- 1/2 bell pepper, sliced
- 1/4 red onion, thinly sliced
- 1/4 cup Kalamata olives, sliced
- 1/4 cup feta cheese, crumbled
- Fresh spinach or lettuce

Instructions:

1. Spread hummus evenly on each tortilla.
2. Layer cucumber, bell pepper, red onion, olives, feta cheese, and spinach on top.
3. Roll up the tortillas and slice them into wraps.
4. Serve immediately or wrap in foil for a packed lunch.

Lemon Garlic Tilapia

Ingredients:

- 2 tilapia fillets
- 2 tbsp olive oil
- 2 cloves garlic, minced
- 1 lemon, sliced
- Salt and pepper to taste
- Fresh parsley for garnish

Instructions:

1. Preheat the oven to 375°F (190°C).
2. Drizzle tilapia fillets with olive oil and season with garlic, salt, and pepper.
3. Place lemon slices on top of the fillets and bake for 15-20 minutes, or until the fish flakes easily.
4. Garnish with fresh parsley and serve with a side of steamed vegetables or rice.

Greek Salad with Grilled Chicken

Ingredients:

- 2 boneless, skinless chicken breasts
- 1 tbsp olive oil
- Salt and pepper to taste
- 1 cucumber, chopped
- 1 cup cherry tomatoes, halved
- 1/2 red onion, sliced
- 1/4 cup Kalamata olives
- 1/4 cup feta cheese, crumbled
- 1 tbsp olive oil (for dressing)
- 1 tbsp red wine vinegar
- 1 tsp dried oregano

Instructions:

1. Preheat the grill to medium-high heat.
2. Season chicken breasts with olive oil, salt, and pepper. Grill for 6-7 minutes per side, until cooked through.
3. In a bowl, combine cucumber, cherry tomatoes, red onion, olives, and feta.
4. In a small bowl, whisk together olive oil, red wine vinegar, oregano, salt, and pepper.
5. Drizzle dressing over the salad and toss to combine.
6. Serve the salad with grilled chicken on top.

Stuffed Bell Peppers with Quinoa and Veggies

Ingredients:

- 4 bell peppers, tops cut off and seeds removed
- 1 cup cooked quinoa
- 1 cup black beans, drained and rinsed
- 1/2 cup corn kernels
- 1/2 onion, chopped
- 1 tsp cumin
- 1 tsp chili powder
- Salt and pepper to taste
- 1/2 cup shredded cheese (optional)

Instructions:

1. Preheat the oven to 375°F (190°C).
2. In a large bowl, combine cooked quinoa, black beans, corn, onion, cumin, chili powder, salt, and pepper.
3. Stuff each bell pepper with the quinoa mixture and place them in a baking dish.
4. Cover with foil and bake for 25 minutes.
5. If using cheese, sprinkle over the stuffed peppers and bake for an additional 5 minutes, until melted.
6. Serve warm.

Sautéed Shrimp with Spinach

Ingredients:

- 1 lb shrimp, peeled and deveined
- 2 tbsp olive oil
- 2 cloves garlic, minced
- 4 cups fresh spinach
- Salt and pepper to taste
- 1 tbsp lemon juice
- Fresh parsley for garnish

Instructions:

1. Heat olive oil in a large pan over medium heat.
2. Add garlic and sauté for 1 minute until fragrant.
3. Add shrimp and cook for 2-3 minutes on each side, until pink and cooked through.
4. Add spinach to the pan and cook for another 2 minutes, until wilted.
5. Season with salt, pepper, and lemon juice.
6. Garnish with fresh parsley and serve.

Grilled Veggie and Hummus Pita

Ingredients:

- 2 whole wheat pitas
- 1/2 cup hummus
- 1 zucchini, sliced
- 1 red bell pepper, sliced
- 1 red onion, sliced
- 1 tbsp olive oil
- Salt and pepper to taste
- Fresh parsley for garnish

Instructions:

1. Preheat the grill to medium heat.
2. Toss zucchini, bell pepper, and onion with olive oil, salt, and pepper.
3. Grill the vegetables for 4-5 minutes on each side, until tender.
4. Warm the pitas on the grill for 1-2 minutes.
5. Spread hummus on the pitas, then top with the grilled veggies.
6. Garnish with fresh parsley and serve.

Baked Eggplant with Tomato and Basil

Ingredients:

- 1 large eggplant, sliced into rounds
- 2 tbsp olive oil
- Salt and pepper to taste
- 1 cup marinara sauce
- 1/2 cup fresh mozzarella, shredded
- Fresh basil leaves

Instructions:

1. Preheat the oven to 400°F (200°C).
2. Arrange eggplant slices on a baking sheet and drizzle with olive oil.
3. Season with salt and pepper, and bake for 20 minutes, flipping halfway through.
4. Spoon marinara sauce over each slice and sprinkle with mozzarella.
5. Return to the oven for 5 minutes, or until cheese is melted.
6. Garnish with fresh basil and serve.

Sweet Potato and Kale Soup

Ingredients:

- 2 medium sweet potatoes, peeled and diced
- 4 cups vegetable broth
- 1 bunch kale, chopped
- 1 onion, chopped
- 2 cloves garlic, minced
- 1 tsp cumin
- Salt and pepper to taste
- 1 tbsp olive oil

Instructions:

1. In a large pot, heat olive oil over medium heat.
2. Add onion and garlic, and sauté for 5 minutes until softened.
3. Add sweet potatoes, vegetable broth, cumin, salt, and pepper.
4. Bring to a boil, then reduce heat and simmer for 20 minutes until sweet potatoes are tender.
5. Stir in the kale and cook for another 5 minutes.
6. Blend the soup until smooth, if desired. Serve warm.

Broccoli and Almond Salad

Ingredients:

- 4 cups broccoli florets, steamed
- 1/4 cup sliced almonds, toasted
- 1/4 red onion, thinly sliced
- 1/2 cup feta cheese, crumbled
- 2 tbsp olive oil
- 1 tbsp apple cider vinegar
- 1 tsp honey
- Salt and pepper to taste

Instructions:

1. Steam broccoli florets until tender, about 5-7 minutes.
2. In a large bowl, combine broccoli, toasted almonds, red onion, and feta.
3. In a small bowl, whisk together olive oil, vinegar, honey, salt, and pepper.
4. Drizzle dressing over the salad and toss to combine.
5. Serve chilled or at room temperature.

Grilled Lemon Chicken with Steamed Broccoli

Ingredients:

- 2 boneless, skinless chicken breasts
- 1 tbsp olive oil
- Juice of 1 lemon
- 1 tsp garlic powder
- Salt and pepper to taste
- 2 cups broccoli florets, steamed

Instructions:

1. Preheat the grill to medium-high heat.
2. In a bowl, combine olive oil, lemon juice, garlic powder, salt, and pepper.
3. Coat chicken breasts in the marinade and let sit for 10-15 minutes.
4. Grill chicken for 6-7 minutes on each side, or until cooked through.
5. Steam broccoli florets for 5-7 minutes.
6. Serve the grilled chicken with steamed broccoli on the side.

Zesty Tomato and Basil Soup

Ingredients:

- 4 cups canned diced tomatoes
- 1 onion, chopped
- 2 cloves garlic, minced
- 1 tsp dried basil
- 1 tbsp olive oil
- Salt and pepper to taste
- 1/2 cup fresh basil leaves, chopped
- 1 cup vegetable broth

Instructions:

1. In a large pot, heat olive oil over medium heat.
2. Add onion and garlic, and sauté for 5 minutes until softened.
3. Add diced tomatoes, basil, salt, and pepper.
4. Stir in vegetable broth and bring to a boil.
5. Reduce heat and simmer for 10 minutes.
6. Blend the soup until smooth, then stir in fresh basil.
7. Serve hot with a drizzle of olive oil.

Cauliflower and Broccoli Fritters

Ingredients:

- 1 cup cauliflower florets, steamed
- 1 cup broccoli florets, steamed
- 1/2 cup breadcrumbs
- 1/4 cup Parmesan cheese, grated
- 1 egg
- 2 tbsp olive oil
- Salt and pepper to taste

Instructions:

1. Preheat the oven to 375°F (190°C).
2. Mash cauliflower and broccoli in a bowl until mostly smooth.
3. Stir in breadcrumbs, Parmesan, egg, salt, and pepper.
4. Form the mixture into small patties.
5. Heat olive oil in a pan over medium heat and cook fritters for 2-3 minutes on each side, until golden.
6. Transfer fritters to a baking sheet and bake for 10 minutes, or until crispy.
7. Serve warm.

Grilled Salmon with Avocado Salsa

Ingredients:

- 2 salmon fillets
- 1 tbsp olive oil
- Salt and pepper to taste
- 1 avocado, diced
- 1/4 cup red onion, finely chopped
- 1/2 cup cherry tomatoes, diced
- 1 tbsp cilantro, chopped
- Juice of 1 lime

Instructions:

1. Preheat the grill to medium-high heat.
2. Season salmon fillets with olive oil, salt, and pepper.
3. Grill salmon for 4-5 minutes on each side, or until cooked through.
4. In a bowl, combine avocado, red onion, tomatoes, cilantro, and lime juice.
5. Serve the grilled salmon topped with avocado salsa.

Tofu Stir-Fry with Veggies

Ingredients:

- 1 block firm tofu, drained and cubed
- 2 tbsp sesame oil
- 1 bell pepper, sliced
- 1 cup broccoli florets
- 1 carrot, julienned
- 1/2 onion, sliced
- 2 cloves garlic, minced
- 2 tbsp soy sauce
- 1 tbsp rice vinegar
- 1 tbsp honey (optional)
- 1 tbsp sesame seeds
- Fresh cilantro for garnish

Instructions:

1. Press tofu to remove excess moisture, then cut into cubes.
2. Heat sesame oil in a large pan over medium-high heat.
3. Add tofu cubes and cook until golden brown on all sides, about 5-7 minutes.
4. Add garlic, onion, bell pepper, broccoli, and carrot, and stir-fry for another 5-7 minutes, until vegetables are tender.
5. Stir in soy sauce, rice vinegar, and honey (if using), and cook for another 2 minutes.
6. Sprinkle with sesame seeds and fresh cilantro before serving.

Cabbage and Bean Soup

Ingredients:

- 4 cups vegetable broth
- 1/2 head cabbage, shredded
- 1 can (15 oz) white beans, drained and rinsed
- 1 carrot, chopped
- 1 onion, chopped
- 2 cloves garlic, minced
- 1 tsp dried thyme
- Salt and pepper to taste
- 1 tbsp olive oil

Instructions:

1. In a large pot, heat olive oil over medium heat.
2. Add onion, carrot, and garlic, and sauté for 5 minutes until softened.
3. Stir in cabbage, vegetable broth, white beans, thyme, salt, and pepper.
4. Bring to a boil, then reduce the heat and simmer for 20 minutes until the cabbage is tender.
5. Taste and adjust seasoning as needed. Serve hot.

Lemon Herb Grilled Vegetables

Ingredients:

- 1 zucchini, sliced
- 1 bell pepper, sliced
- 1 red onion, sliced
- 1 cup cherry tomatoes, halved
- 2 tbsp olive oil
- Juice of 1 lemon
- 1 tbsp fresh thyme, chopped
- 1 tbsp fresh parsley, chopped
- Salt and pepper to taste

Instructions:

1. Preheat the grill to medium-high heat.
2. Toss vegetables with olive oil, lemon juice, thyme, parsley, salt, and pepper.
3. Grill vegetables for 3-4 minutes on each side, until tender and lightly charred.
4. Serve hot, garnished with extra herbs.

Turkey Chili

Ingredients:

- 1 lb ground turkey
- 1 onion, chopped
- 2 cloves garlic, minced
- 1 can (15 oz) kidney beans, drained and rinsed
- 1 can (15 oz) black beans, drained and rinsed
- 1 can (15 oz) diced tomatoes
- 1 tbsp chili powder
- 1 tsp cumin
- 1 tsp smoked paprika
- Salt and pepper to taste
- 1 tbsp olive oil

Instructions:

1. Heat olive oil in a large pot over medium heat.
2. Add ground turkey, onion, and garlic, and cook until turkey is browned and onions are softened, about 7 minutes.
3. Stir in beans, tomatoes, chili powder, cumin, smoked paprika, salt, and pepper.
4. Bring to a boil, then reduce heat and simmer for 20 minutes.
5. Serve hot, topped with your favorite chili toppings (cheese, sour cream, cilantro).

Spinach and Feta Stuffed Chicken Breast

Ingredients:

- 4 boneless, skinless chicken breasts
- 2 cups fresh spinach
- 1/2 cup feta cheese, crumbled
- 1/4 cup cream cheese, softened
- 1 tbsp olive oil
- Salt and pepper to taste
- 1 tsp garlic powder

Instructions:

1. Preheat the oven to 375°F (190°C).
2. In a pan, sauté spinach until wilted, about 3-4 minutes.
3. In a bowl, combine spinach, feta cheese, and cream cheese.
4. Cut a slit in each chicken breast to create a pocket.
5. Stuff the chicken breasts with the spinach and feta mixture, and secure with toothpicks.
6. Heat olive oil in a pan over medium-high heat and sear the chicken for 2-3 minutes on each side until golden.
7. Transfer chicken to the oven and bake for 20-25 minutes, until cooked through.
8. Serve hot.

Carrot and Ginger Soup

Ingredients:

- 4 large carrots, peeled and chopped
- 1 onion, chopped
- 1 tbsp fresh ginger, grated
- 4 cups vegetable broth
- 2 tbsp olive oil
- Salt and pepper to taste
- 1/2 cup coconut milk (optional)

Instructions:

1. Heat olive oil in a large pot over medium heat.
2. Add onion and ginger, and sauté for 5 minutes until softened.
3. Add carrots and vegetable broth, and bring to a boil.
4. Reduce heat and simmer for 20 minutes, until carrots are tender.
5. Blend the soup until smooth using an immersion blender or regular blender.
6. Stir in coconut milk, salt, and pepper.
7. Serve warm.

Roasted Beet and Goat Cheese Salad

Ingredients:

- 2 medium beets, roasted and sliced
- 4 cups mixed greens
- 1/4 cup goat cheese, crumbled
- 1/4 cup walnuts, toasted
- 1/4 cup balsamic vinegar
- 2 tbsp olive oil
- Salt and pepper to taste

Instructions:

1. Preheat the oven to 400°F (200°C).
2. Roast beets in foil for 45-60 minutes until tender, then peel and slice.
3. In a bowl, toss mixed greens with balsamic vinegar, olive oil, salt, and pepper.
4. Top with roasted beets, goat cheese, and toasted walnuts.
5. Serve immediately.

Sautéed Spinach and Garlic with Lemon

Ingredients:

- 4 cups fresh spinach
- 2 cloves garlic, minced
- 1 tbsp olive oil
- Juice of 1 lemon
- Salt and pepper to taste

Instructions:

1. Heat olive oil in a pan over medium heat.
2. Add garlic and sauté for 1 minute until fragrant.
3. Add spinach and sauté for 3-4 minutes until wilted.
4. Drizzle with lemon juice and season with salt and pepper.
5. Serve warm.

Light Chicken Fajitas

Ingredients:

- 2 chicken breasts, thinly sliced
- 1 red bell pepper, sliced
- 1 green bell pepper, sliced
- 1 onion, sliced
- 1 tbsp olive oil
- 1 tsp chili powder
- 1 tsp cumin
- 1 tsp garlic powder
- Salt and pepper to taste
- Juice of 1 lime
- 4 small whole wheat tortillas
- Fresh cilantro, for garnish

Instructions:

1. Heat olive oil in a large pan over medium heat.
2. Add chicken and cook until browned and cooked through, about 5-7 minutes.
3. Add the sliced bell peppers and onion, and cook for an additional 5 minutes, until vegetables are tender.
4. Season with chili powder, cumin, garlic powder, salt, and pepper.
5. Squeeze lime juice over the mixture and toss to combine.
6. Warm the tortillas in a separate pan or microwave.
7. Serve the chicken and vegetable mixture in tortillas, garnished with fresh cilantro.

Baked Cod with Veggie Medley

Ingredients:

- 4 cod fillets
- 1 tbsp olive oil
- 1 lemon, sliced
- 1 cup cherry tomatoes, halved
- 1 zucchini, sliced
- 1 red bell pepper, sliced
- 1 tsp dried oregano
- Salt and pepper to taste

Instructions:

1. Preheat the oven to 400°F (200°C).
2. Arrange cod fillets on a baking sheet lined with parchment paper.
3. Drizzle with olive oil, and season with salt, pepper, and dried oregano.
4. Scatter lemon slices, tomatoes, zucchini, and bell pepper around the cod fillets.
5. Bake for 15-20 minutes, until the cod is cooked through and flakes easily with a fork.
6. Serve the cod and roasted vegetables hot.

Grilled Shrimp with Cucumber Relish

Ingredients:

- 1 lb large shrimp, peeled and deveined
- 1 tbsp olive oil
- Juice of 1 lime
- 1 tbsp chili powder
- Salt and pepper to taste
- 1 cucumber, diced
- 1/4 cup red onion, finely chopped
- 1 tbsp fresh cilantro, chopped
- 1 tbsp rice vinegar

Instructions:

1. In a bowl, toss shrimp with olive oil, lime juice, chili powder, salt, and pepper.
2. Preheat the grill to medium-high heat and thread shrimp onto skewers.
3. Grill shrimp for 2-3 minutes on each side until cooked through.
4. For the relish, combine diced cucumber, red onion, cilantro, and rice vinegar in a small bowl.
5. Serve the grilled shrimp with a generous spoonful of cucumber relish on top.

Spicy Chicken and Cabbage Stir-Fry

Ingredients:

- 2 chicken breasts, thinly sliced
- 1/2 small head of cabbage, shredded
- 2 tbsp sesame oil
- 1 red bell pepper, sliced
- 2 cloves garlic, minced
- 1 tbsp ginger, minced
- 2 tbsp soy sauce
- 1 tbsp sriracha sauce (adjust to taste)
- 1 tbsp rice vinegar
- Salt and pepper to taste

Instructions:

1. Heat sesame oil in a large pan or wok over medium-high heat.
2. Add chicken and cook until browned, about 5-7 minutes.
3. Add garlic, ginger, and bell pepper, and stir-fry for 2-3 minutes.
4. Stir in shredded cabbage, soy sauce, sriracha sauce, and rice vinegar.
5. Continue to stir-fry until the cabbage is tender, about 5 more minutes.
6. Season with salt and pepper, and serve hot.

Cauliflower and Lentil Stew

Ingredients:

- 1 head cauliflower, cut into florets
- 1 cup green lentils, rinsed
- 1 onion, chopped
- 2 cloves garlic, minced
- 2 carrots, chopped
- 2 tbsp olive oil
- 1 can (14 oz) diced tomatoes
- 4 cups vegetable broth
- 1 tsp cumin
- 1 tsp turmeric
- Salt and pepper to taste

Instructions:

1. Heat olive oil in a large pot over medium heat.
2. Add onion, garlic, and carrots, and sauté until softened, about 5 minutes.
3. Stir in cumin, turmeric, salt, and pepper, and cook for 1 more minute.
4. Add cauliflower, lentils, diced tomatoes, and vegetable broth.
5. Bring to a boil, then reduce heat and simmer for 30 minutes, or until the lentils and cauliflower are tender.
6. Adjust seasoning and serve hot.

Grilled Tuna Salad with Lime Vinaigrette

Ingredients:

- 2 tuna steaks
- 1 tbsp olive oil
- Salt and pepper to taste
- 4 cups mixed greens
- 1 avocado, sliced
- 1/4 red onion, thinly sliced
- 1/2 cucumber, sliced
- 1 tbsp fresh cilantro, chopped

For the vinaigrette:

- 2 tbsp olive oil
- Juice of 1 lime
- 1 tsp honey
- 1 tsp Dijon mustard
- Salt and pepper to taste

Instructions:

1. Preheat the grill to medium-high heat.
2. Brush tuna steaks with olive oil, and season with salt and pepper.
3. Grill tuna for 3-4 minutes on each side for medium-rare, or longer to your desired doneness.
4. In a small bowl, whisk together olive oil, lime juice, honey, Dijon mustard, salt, and pepper to make the vinaigrette.
5. Toss mixed greens, avocado, onion, cucumber, and cilantro in a large bowl.
6. Slice grilled tuna and arrange on top of the salad.
7. Drizzle with lime vinaigrette and serve immediately.

www.ingramcontent.com/pod-product-compliance
Lightning Source LLC
LaVergne TN
LVHW081341060526
838201LV00055B/2785